Kamden Faith Journey Series, Book 6

I0141986

Kindness

Tamika Champion-Hampton

Energion Publications
Gonzalez, Florida
2019

Cover Image: Amanda Martinez

ISBN13: 978-1-63199-741-9
eISBN: 978-1-63199-742-6

Energion Publications
P. O. Box 841
Gonzalez, FL 32560

energion.com
pubs@energion.com

bul·ly·ing — to treat someone in a cruel, insulting, threatening, or aggressive manner; to cause someone to do something by means of force or coercion

One bright and sunny day, Nana noticed Kamden looking out the window towards the park.

"Would you like to go to the park?" she asked.

Kamden just kept staring out of the window. "No ma'am, Nana, I don't want to go."
Nana shrugged her shoulders and went back to her sewing.

As the morning wore on and became day, Kamden continued to look out of the window. "Kamden, are you sure you don't want to go to the park? I see you watching the other kids having so much fun!

Kamden turned around. "Nana, I do want to go play. Could you come with me?" he said quietly.

"Well, yes I can for a little while." Nana said with a smile.

As they were walking to the park, Chloe and Kia were also out and coming towards them. "Hey, Kamden! Hey, Nana!" the girls yelled.

"Hey, darlings!" said Nana.

Chloe took Kamden by the hand and said,
"Come on, Kamden! Let's play!"
Hours went by as they played and played.

Nana noticed a little boy named Ryan, looking
very angry.

"What's wrong, young man?" Nana asked Ryan.

"I am mad and I don't like anyone!" and he
stormed off.

When it was time to go home, Nana called for Kamden.
"Let's go, Kamden! It's time to go!"

As they were walking home, Nana noticed that Ryan was again by himself, stomping around like he was still angry.

Nana turned and went over to put her arm around Kamden. "Do you know Ryan, Kamden?"

"Yes Nana, I do." Kamden said quietly. "He is very mean to some of the kids at the playground."

"Really?" said Nana. Her eyes looked surprised.

Kamden nodded his head. "Nana, he hits and makes fun of us. He makes us cry! I really like going to the playground but Ryan makes it so hard to have a good time."

Kamden looked down at the ground and then back at Nana. "Nana? What am I supposed to do about him?"

Nana and Kamden walked up to the front door of the house and stopped there. Nana took Kamden's hand and sat down close to him in the chair on the patio.

"Kamden, one thing for sure we must do is pray for him. And another thing-- show yourself to be friendly in the meantime. If Ryan tries to hit you or other kids, please tell an adult. My precious boy, all you can do is be nice to him and play with him if you can."

Kamden just shook his head.
"Nana, why is he like that?" asked Kamden.

Nana smiled sadly and said, "Things in his life may not be good and he probably doesn't understand why." She went on, "When someone his own age is around him, Ryan remembers his own pain and he wants everyone else to feel like he does: scared, angry and afraid."

Nana held Kamden's hand tight and continued, "What you need to do is show compassion to him and show him how to have fun; then he will come around and want to play like you do, so you and everyone else will want to play together too!"

The next day came and it was time to go to the playground. There was Ryan standing all alone and Kamden went over and asked him if he wanted to play with them.
He gave a shy "Yes" and they played and had great fun together.

amden ran home that afternoon yelling, "Nana! Jana! Ryan is really not that bad! He had some un playing and running around today with all of s!"

Good, Kamden." said Nana. "Sometimes we have to understand how the other person feels. am so proud of you, Kamden. You made a ew friend today and showed Ryan how to be a riend too."

Previous books:
Salvation
The Gathering
What Is Love?
Friendship
The Birth

Check https://energiondirect.com/product-category/kamden-faith-journey/ for more information, or point your smartphone camera at the QR code below.

www.ingramcontent.com/pod-product-compliance
Lightning Source LLC
LaVergne TN
LVHW070835080426
835508LV00031B/3478